DEBBIE FORWARD

Help Your Child Learn to Read

Nurturing Young Minds: A Parent's Guide to Fun and Easy Activities That Will Help Build Reading Readiness Skills and Empower Your Child for School Success

Jared,
I can't wait listen to you read at Jefferson
☆ Mrs. Forward

Copyright © 2023 by Debbie Forward

All rights reserved. No part of this publication may be reproduced, stored or transmitted in any form or by any means, electronic, mechanical, photocopying, recording, scanning, or otherwise without written permission from the publisher. It is illegal to copy this book, post it to a website, or distribute it by any other means without permission.

Debbie Forward asserts the moral right to be identified as the author of this work.

Debbie Forward has no responsibility for the persistence or accuracy of URLs for external or third-party Internet Websites referred to in this publication and does not guarantee that any content on such Websites is, or will remain, accurate or appropriate.

Designations used by companies to distinguish their products are often claimed as trademarks. All brand names and product names used in this book and on its cover are trade names, service marks, trademarks and registered trademarks of their respective owners. The publishers and the book are not associated with any product or vendor mentioned in this book. None of the companies referenced within the book have endorsed the book.

First edition

This book was professionally typeset on Reedsy.
Find out more at reedsy.com

To my beloved children and cherished students,
This book is dedicated to the joy of reading that we've shared. May the stories we've explored together serve as a reminder of the beauty, wisdom, and unity that can be found within the pages of a book.

"We may not be able to prepare the future for our children, but we can at least prepare our children for the future."

-Franklin D. Roosevelt

Contents

1	Introduction	1
2	Building a Foundation	4
3	Fun and Easy Phonological/Phonemic Awareness Activities	16
4	Fun and Easy Phonics Activities	20
5	Fun and Easy Fluency Activities	25
6	Fun and Easy Vocabulary Activities	33
7	Fun and Easy Comprehension Activities	36
8	Building a Love of Reading and Learning	39
9	Conclusion	44
10	References	46
	About the Author	48

1

Introduction

"A love of learning has a lot to do with learning that we are loved."
— *Fred Rogers*

Welcome to <u>Help Your Child Learn to Read!</u> My name is Debbie Forward, and I'm extremely excited to be writing this book. Having been an elementary teacher for thirty years, children's literacy is a subject that is very close to my heart. Teaching has been my life's work, and it has brought me so much joy. There really is nothing better than watching a child start to see themselves as a learner and feel successful. The look on a child's face when they start to understand a concept and begin to realize that they are learning is amazing to see.

In my years of teaching, I have been fortunate enough to see this look of success on a student's face countless times. However, on the other hand, I have also seen the look of a struggling student who desperately wants to understand, but just doesn't get it. The student who pays attention and tries hard to learn, but just can't make the connection. This is the part of teaching that makes every teacher wish that they had a magic wand that they could just wave over the student's head and make them magically understand and learn with ease. Unfortunately, teachers do not possess magic powers. Although, after working with hundreds of students and their families, I have come to believe that **parents do have magic powers when it comes to their child's success with learning to read.** The magic that can open the doors to learning and truly make the difference between the child who easily learns to read and the child who struggles simply comes from building a literacy-rich environment at home. Spending time reading with your child everyday, playing learning games, talking with your child, and helping them observe and discover the world around them are all excellent ways to empower your child for school success and unleash the magic of learning that will last their lifetime.

If you are reading this book, I know that you are dedicated to helping your child learn to read, because you are taking steps to understand how to help your child be successful. This is a great first step! This book is intended to help you along this path and show you how easy and enjoyable the journey to your child's reading success can be. Although I have used many of the ideas in this book in my classroom and with my own four children as they were growing up, I want to be clear that most of these activities are not my original ideas. They are strategies and activities that I have found online. This book is a parent's guide, in which I have compiled information on the building blocks of learning to read and provided activities that support your child's growth in each area. I understand that parents are busy, and it is hard to find the time to research ways to support their young learners. My goal with this book is to provide you with quality information and fun and easy activities, in order to make it easier for you to build a literacy-rich

INTRODUCTION

home environment that will help you nurture your young reader and empower them for school success in Kindergarten and beyond!

2

Building a Foundation

Parents who read 1 picture book with their children every day provide their children with exposure to an estimated 78,000 words each year. Cumulatively, over the 5 years before kindergarten entry, we estimate that children from literacy-rich homes hear a cumulative 1.4 million more words during storybook reading than children who are never read to.
Jessica A. R. Logan, The Ohio State University, Journal of Developmental & Behavioral Pediatrics 40(5):p 383-386, June 2019.

The quote above clearly illustrates the number one way parents can foster reading readiness at home, and it is very easy and extremely enjoyable. It is simply reading to your child and enjoying books together. Isn't it truly amazing that by reading just one book to your child a day you are exposing them to 78,000 words each year? By doing this one simple and enjoyable thing everyday, you are giving your child an amazing head start on their way to learning to read. On the contrary, imagine a child who is not read to at home.

The opposite effect is true. That child is starting at a disadvantage and sadly begins school already behind many other students. However, as I mentioned in the introduction, parents have the power to change this and the ability to empower their child for school success simply by reading to them! It is as easy as that, but there is much more you can do to ignite your child's excitement and love of reading. This chapter will help you understand the basics of reading, the benefits of reading aloud together, how to choose good books for your child and how to develop a consistent routine that incorporates reading into your child's daily life.

Understanding the Basics

We have all, at some point in our lives, learned to read, but most of us don't remember **how** we learned. We might remember the teacher who taught us to read or some of our favorite early books that we were able to read all by ourselves. But, most of us don't even remember a time in our lives that we didn't know how to read. It was just so long ago. The fact that we don't remember how we learned to read can make it difficult for us, as parents, to understand how to help our children learn to read. With this in mind, I have included the five essential building blocks of reading in this chapter, in order to help you better understand the components of reading. The National Institute of Child Health and Human Development has identified the five essential components of reading as: Phonemic Awareness, Phonics, Fluency, Vocabulary, and Comprehension. To become a fluent reader, a child needs to have strong skills in all five areas.

*Phonological Awareness (which includes phonemic awareness)
Phonological/phonemic awareness is really just a fancy term for an easy concept that children begin developing from birth to five years old,

with most children mastering it by the end of first grade. *It is simply the ability to hear, recognize and play with sounds in the spoken language.* For example, hearing the beginning, middle or ending sounds in words, identifying rhyming words, counting the number of syllables in words or counting the number of words in a sentence are all phonological awareness skills. Phonological awareness encompasses sounds, words, and sentences. Whereas, phonemic awareness only involves the sounds within words. Phonemes are simply the individual sounds heard in words. Therefore, phonemic awareness skills help children understand that words are made up of sounds. For example, the word cat has three phonemes (/c/ /a/ /t/). Phonological/phonemic awareness is an auditory skill (hearing), not visual (seeing).

*Phonics

While phonological/phonemic awareness focuses on hearing sounds, phonics combines hearing the sounds and seeing the letters, so it becomes auditory and visual. Hearing the sounds and seeing the letters helps children to build letter/sound correspondence (The ability to identify the letter that represents the sound). **Phonics focuses on letter/sound relationships.** The English language has 44 sounds (phonemes). Phonics helps children blend and segment sounds in order to decode words in reading and encode words in writing.

*Fluency

Fluency in reading is the ability to read text easily. It has four parts; accuracy, speed, expression, and comprehension. Sometimes fluency is just associated with speed, but there is much more involved in it. To be a fluent reader, a child must be able to read the words accurately, use an appropriate amount of speed and expression, and comprehend what is being read.

***Vocabulary**
Vocabulary refers to the words we must know and understand in order to communicate effectively. Oral vocabulary refers to the words we must use and understand in speaking and listening. Reading vocabulary refers to the words we must be able to read and understand in print. Vocabulary is important to reading, because a reader must understand the meaning of the words they are reading, in order to comprehend what is being read.

***Comprehension**
Comprehension is the ability to read text and understand its meaning using information the reader already knows (prior knowledge). Reading comprehension involves connecting the reader's own knowledge and experiences to the information in the text. Comprehension is the ultimate goal of reading. The ability to understand a text is what brings out the learning and joy from the text.

These five building blocks of reading work together to create the reading experience. In order to become a successful reader, children must develop skills in all five areas. In this book, I will provide several fun and simple activities that you can easily incorporate into your child's daily routine that will help to strengthen these areas of your child's cognitive development. I will start with my favorite one, and in my opinion, the most powerful and enjoyable one: Storytime!

Reading Aloud Together

Some of my favorite memories from when my children were small include them snuggling up on my lap and sharing books together. We read so many books over and over. Those memories still bring a smile to my face, because I know that those are great memories for my children, as well. It was a time that we snuggled together, were silly together, laughed together, explored together, learned together and bonded together. There are so many benefits to reading aloud together, not only for your child, but also for you!

Benefits for your child:

- Helps to develop first literacy skills by building your child's knowledge of letters, words, sentences.
- Builds vocabulary and improves language skills
- Develops listening and comprehension skills
- Strengthens attention span
- Builds learning concepts, such as before/after, cause/effect, problem/solution
- Helps children learn about the world around them
- Strengthens values, such as empathy and helping others
- Encourages creativity and imagination
- Develops a sense of well-being and supports a strong child/parent relationship.
- Cultivates a lifelong love of reading and learning

Benefits for the parent:

- Builds a sense of connection with your child
- Provides a great way for a family to spend time together
- Reduces stress and helps you to wind down after a hectic day
- Help you build a bedtime routine for your child
- Builds family memories and traditions
- Promotes laughter and positive emotions

Wow, that is quite a list! I am sure you would agree that the benefits of spending 20 minutes a day reading with your child are enormous and can make such a difference in your child's overall well-being and cognitive development. By consistently doing this one enjoyable activity, you can give your child a huge jump start on their way to becoming a reader, which will ultimately have a great impact on their overall school success.

Your next questions might be, "At what age should I start reading to my child?" and "How do I choose the right books for my child?" Both are great questions. The answer to the first question is NOW! If you haven't already, you should start reading to your child right away. Even babies benefit from reading together. Being held close and hearing the voice of a loved one gives a baby a sense of well-being and starts them on the path to learning. According to Carolyn Cates, PhD, lead author and research assistant professor in the department of pediatrics at New York University (NYU) School of Medicine, "Reading to young children, beginning even in early infancy, has a lasting effect on language, literacy and early reading skills,"

Here are some suggestions to answer the second question, "How do I choose the right books for my child?":

Infants and Toddlers: Children of this age are best engaged by books that have the following characteristics:

- Sturdy covers and pages, such as hard cardboard books (board books), soft vinyl or plastic books and fabric books
- Interactive books with handles, flaps, textured pages and sound effects
- Bright colors and patterns

- Simple illustrations
- Rhyming and repetitive text

Preschoolers: The article, "8 Tips for Choosing Books for Kids" (readingegg.com) suggests these tips to help parents choose books for children 2 to 5 years old:

1. Choose good books that are easy to relate to

Choose books that allow your child to explore different worlds and lives but are still familiar enough that they can see themselves in the characters. Even if it's a story set in an imaginary world of monsters and fairies, if the characters have hopes and desires that are easy to relate to, your child will be more interested in reading it until the end.

2. Opt for books that teach kids important things

Whether it's learning a timeless moral in *The Tortoise and the Hare* or learning about numbers, fruit, and days of the week in *The Very Hungry Caterpillar*, the best books often teach things without us even realizing it. Choose books that deliver an important message or subtly teach essential skills such as the alphabet, counting, colors, or seasons.

3. Choose books that may not be your personal pick

Children's author Libby Gleeson suggests that when choosing a good book for children, parents should "resist the desire only to feed their children the books they loved when they were young". Your child may not share the same passion for your childhood classics, and, as Gleeson notes, "The world has changed and children have changed."

4. Find books that are not too difficult to read for kids

Use the Five Finger Rule if your child will be reading on their own. [Hold up one finger for each word your child doesn't know, if you get to five fingers, the book is probably too difficult for your child to read.] If the book has a few difficult words, read it aloud together with your child. There's nothing wrong with exposing children to more complex language in context. But if you know the language and concepts will be too difficult for them to enjoy the story, avoid putting them off reading altogether by choosing a simpler book.

5. Look for kids' books with strong illustrations

Vivid and clear imagery that supports the story is powerful for early readers. Choose books that have good illustrations that correspond with the storyline. Wordless books are also a great way to develop your child's language skills, as they require readers to interpret the illustrations as the story progresses.

6. Choose books that are fun to read aloud

How many times has your child requested yet another reading of *Dr Seuss*? Books that rhyme or have a good lyrical flow are fun to read aloud and listen to. Read with enthusiasm and use different voices for different characters to bring the reading experience to life.

7. Look into kids' books that are trending

Talk to your child's teacher, librarian, or other parents to find out about popular children's books. Alternatively, search online for award-winning children's book lists or hop onto book review sites to read what other parents are suggesting. Jump on TikTok and check out what's trending.

8. Good books can simply be the books your child desires

At the end of the day, what makes a good children's book is any age-appropriate book your child wants to read! Let your child choose which books they would like to read because choosing to read over not choosing to read is a significant step towards a lifelong love of reading.

I hope these tips were helpful, but please don't stress yourself out over which books are best for your child. The quality of the time spent reading with your child is way more important than book choice or if it is a good fit book for your child. You are a good fit parent for your child, and you are regularly spending time reading with your child. That's all that really matters and that's what is going to make the difference in your child's life.

While the quality of reading time with your child is important, quantity is also important. In order for your child to receive the best benefits, you have to be consistent and read to them often. Reading together should be fun and frequent. It should be part of your daily routine. In my family, it worked best to make storytime a part of my children's bedtime routine. After they brushed their teeth and put on their pajamas, they would always grab a few books and climb into my bed. We would snuggle together reading and rereading all their favorite books. Some nights, I was tired and didn't really want to read, but they were always excited about it. Seeing the excitement about reading in their sweet little faces told me I couldn't skip storytime! As I tucked them into their own beds each night, I always felt the sense of connection that reading together had given us, and I went to bed each night knowing that my children felt that connection also. Reading together truly is magical!

That is the routine that worked best for my family, but every family is different and therefore, might need a different routine. In his article, "Creative Ways to Incorporate Reading into Your Child's Daily Routine", Michael Anderson suggests the following ideas:

Make reading part of your bedtime routine

Many children look forward to being read to before bed, and it can be a great way to wind down after a busy day. Choose a book that your child is interested in and take turns reading a few pages each night. You can also encourage your child to read to you.

Turn reading into a game

Children love to play games, and you can turn reading into a game by creating a scavenger hunt. Write clues on pieces of paper and hide them around the house. Each clue should lead to the next one and the final clue should lead to a prize. You can also create a reading race, where your child has to read a certain number of pages in a certain amount of time.

Read together as a family

Set aside a specific time each week for your family to read together. You can choose a book that everyone can read or take turns reading aloud to each other. Reading together as a family can be a great bonding activity and can also encourage your child to read more.

Make reading a reward

Use reading as a reward for good behavior or completing chores. For example, if your child finishes their homework on time, they can choose a book to read for a certain amount of time. This can help your child see reading as a fun and enjoyable activity rather than a chore.

Take advantage of waiting time

There are often times during the day when your child has to wait, such as at the doctor's office or in the car. Encourage your child to bring a book with them and read during these times. This can help make waiting time more enjoyable for your child and can also improve their reading skills.

Encourage independent reading

It is important for children to develop the habit of reading independently, and you can encourage this by setting aside a specific time each day for your child to read on their own. You can also create a cozy reading nook in your home with comfortable seating and plenty of books.

Read with technology

Many children enjoy using technology, and there are several ways you can incorporate reading with technology into your child's daily routine. You can download e-books onto a tablet or smartphone, or you can use reading apps that provide interactive reading experiences. Just be sure to set limits on screen time.

As you read through these ideas, please keep in mind that reading will look different for preschoolers. They aren't quite ready to read the words, so they might be picture reading or pretend reading. This is an important first step in becoming a reader and helps to build many important skills, such as language and critical thinking skills. Pretend reading also builds children's confidence and helps them to see themselves as readers, which is so important.

In this chapter, I hope that you were able to see that, as a parent, you hold the key to empowering your child to be a successful learner. Did you know that 90% of your child's brain is developed by 5 years old? Therefore, you are your child's first and most important teacher. This chapter highlighted the basics of reading and the importance of reading aloud together, as well as, how to choose good fit books and how to create a consistent reading routine for your child. In the next chapters, I will show you some fun and easy activities that will help your child develop skills in all five of the essential reading components listed in this chapter.

If you keep your eyes open enough, oh, the stuff you will learn.
-Dr. Seuss

3

Fun and Easy Phonological/Phonemic Awareness Activities

*The two biggest predictors of early reading success are alphabet knowledge
and phonemic awareness.*
- Dr. Mary Jager Adams, cognitive and developmental psychologist

This chapter will highlight fun and easy learning activities that you can enjoy with your child that will develop and strengthen their phonological and phonemic awareness skills. Remember, phonological awareness is the ability to hear, recognize and play with sounds in the spoken language at the letter, word and sentence level, while phonemic awareness only includes the sounds within a word.

My first grade students and I had so much fun with phonemic awareness activities in our classroom. Children just naturally love these activities. That is because they are fun! Singing songs, making silly rhymes, clapping out words and making nonsense words are all things kids love to do. They are learning in such a fun way, it doesn't even seem like learning. To the kids, they are just having fun. To

FUN AND EASY PHONOLOGICAL/PHONEMIC AWARENESS ACTIVITIES

help you and your child enjoy this fun way of learning, here are a few phonological/phonemic awareness activities for you to enjoy with your child at home from the article, "Reading 101: A Guide For Parents" (https://www.readingrockets.org).

*Rhyme time

"I am thinking of an animal that rhymes with *big*. What's the animal?" Answer: *pig*. What else rhymes with *big*? (*dig, fig, wig*)

*Body part rhymes

Point to a part of your body and ask your child to think of a rhyming word. For example, what rhymes with *hair*? (*bear*). What rhymes with *eye*? (*pie*) What rhymes with *head*? (*bed*). Make it more challenging by asking for two or three rhyming words. Nonsense words count, too!

*Read books that play with sounds

Try these books featuring rhyme, alliteration and more:

- All About Arthur (An Absolutely Absurd Ape)
- Alphabears
- Animalia
- Buzz Said the Bee
- Catch a Little Fox
- Each Peach Pear Plum
- A Giraffe and a Half
- The Hungry Thing
- Jamberry
- See You Later Alligator
- Sheep in a Jeep
- Yours Till Banana Splits
- Zoophabets

*Clap it out

Practice listening for syllables. Explain to your child that syllables are the big chunks in words as you say them: some words have one syllable (hat), some have two (apple), and some have three or more (banana).

You can actually feel syllables! Have your child put her hand under her chin and say the word slowly so she can feel when her mouth goes down. Be sure to explain that each time her chin goes down, she's saying another syllable or part of the same word.

Think of everyday words your child knows (for example: apple, baby, toothbrush). Tell your child that you'll both clap the number of syllables in each word. Show her how to clap one time as you say each syllable: /ap/ (clap) /ple/ (clap). Try it with more words. Kids also love clapping their name!

*Tongue ticklers

Alliteration or "tongue ticklers" (where the sound you're focusing on is repeated over and over again) can be a fun way to provide practice with a sound. Try these:

For M: Miss Mouse makes marvelous meatballs!
For S: Silly Sally sings songs about snakes and snails.
For F: Freddy finds fireflies with a flashlight.

*"I Spy" first sounds

Practice beginning sounds with this simple "I spy" game at home, on a walk, or at the grocery store. Choose words with distinctive, easy-to-hear beginning sounds. For example, if you're in the bathroom you can say, "I spy something red that starts with the "s" /ssss/ sound (soap)."

*Sound scavenger hunt

Choose a letter sound, then have your child find things around your house that start with the same sound. "Can you find something in our house that starts with the letter "p" /pppp/ sound?" (Picture, pencil, pear)

These are just some of the many phonological/phonemic awareness activities you can find online. By playing games like these that focus on rhyming, alliteration, syllables and letter sounds, you can make a big difference in your child's cognitive development and reading readiness.

In this chapter, I hope you were able to see the value in playing games that help your child to hear, recognize and play with sounds. Playing these games everyday is a simple and fun way to strengthen your child's literacy skills and prepare them for school success.

"Knowledge will bring you the opportunity to make a difference."
-Dr. Seuss

4

Fun and Easy Phonics Activities

"If a child memorized ten words, the child can only read ten words, but if a child learns the sounds of ten letters, the child will be able to read 350 three-sound words, 4,320 four-sound words, and 21,650 five-sound words."
-Dr. Martin Kozloff (2022)

One of my favorite things about teaching first grade is watching a child as they begin to learn to decode words. By first grade, most students know letters and sounds, and many have already started to decode words and are beginning to read. However, there are also students who haven't "cracked the code" to reading yet. Charlie was one of those students. He knew the letter sounds and even a few sight words, but he hadn't quite figured out how to blend sounds together into words. I remember watching him as he said each sound slowly (/h/ /a/ /t/), not sure what he was supposed to be listening for. Then all of a sudden, he heard the word "hat" as he blended the sounds together. He shouted, "Those letters say hat!" Charlie had learned to decode words. He now understood that when he blended the sounds together they would form a word. Strong phonics skills help children decode words.

This chapter will highlight fun and easy activities that you can enjoy with your child that will develop and strengthen your child's phonics skills. This is when your child will start to understand the relationship between sounds and letters. When a child builds letter/sound correspondence and starts to understand that letter symbols represent the sounds heard in words, they are able to begin decoding words. The ability to decode words makes them a reader.

The quote above clearly points out the value in learning letter/sound correspondence and being able to use letter knowledge to decode words. If a child memorizes ten words, then they can only read those ten words. However, if the child knows ten sounds, they can then apply that letter/sound knowledge to other words containing those same letters allowing them to read many, many more words. That is why it is so important to give your child experiences that help them gain letter and sound knowledge. Here are a few fun and interactive activities for you to enjoy with your child from the article, "Teaching Phonics at Home: A Guide for Parents", (https://appbooka.com/blog/teaching-phonics-at-home).

*Silly Sound Safari

For this fun phonics activity, create a scavenger hunt where your child has to locate objects that start with a specific sound. For example, if you're focusing on the letter "B," challenge them to find a banana, a bumblebee, or perhaps even a band of boisterous baboons (okay, maybe not the last one). This game will have them giggling their way to phonics mastery.

*Alphabet Aerobics

Who says learning (and teaching phonics) can't be a workout? Turn phonics into a physical activity by doing the alphabet aerobics. Assign each letter a unique action and then spell out simple words or sounds together. For instance, when you say "cat," everyone jumps like a cat, "dog" triggers enthusiastic tail-wagging, and "zebra" encourages wild galloping across the room. Remember to stretch those muscles before engaging in some serious phonics fitness!

*Rap It, Clap It

Phonics and rhythm go together like peanut butter and jelly. Turn your living room into a hip-hop stage and transform phonics lessons into a rap performance. Choose a letter or sound and create a catchy rap song around it. Throw in some snazzy dance moves, and let your kids be the phonics rockstars they were born to be. Who knows, you might discover the next big phonics prodigy!

*Storytime with a Twist

Unleash your inner storyteller and weave tales that revolve around phonics. Get creative with characters whose names start with the letter you're focusing on. Imagine a courageous cat named Cassidy who conquers crocodiles or a daring dog named Dennis who defies gravity. As you share these stories, emphasize the letter sounds, and encourage your kids to join in. Soon enough, they'll be begging for "one more story, pleeease!"

*Scrabble Shenanigans

It's time to dust off that old Scrabble board and give it a phonics twist. Challenge your child to create words using the letters they have, but with a phonics rule in mind. For example, they can only use words with a specific vowel sound or words that start with a particular consonant blend. Not only will they be sharpening their phonics skills, but you might also stumble upon some hilarious made-up words worthy of the Oxford dictionary.

*Teaching Phonics with an Obstacle Course

Set up a phonics-themed obstacle course in your living room or backyard. Create stations that represent different sounds or phonics patterns. For example, one station could have objects that start with the letter "b," while another station might have words with a specific vowel sound. Encourage your child to navigate the course, correctly identifying and pronouncing each sound or word at each station.

*Word Building with Play Dough

Combine the tactile experience of play dough with word building. Give your child a variety of play dough colors and letter stamps or plastic letter cutters. Provide them with a word or a set of phonics patterns and challenge them to create each word by stamping or cutting out the corresponding letters from the play dough. This activity not only reinforces letter-sound associations but also enhances fine motor skills.

*Rhyming Riddles for Teaching Phonics

Engage your child's creativity and critical thinking skills with rhyming riddles. Give them clues in the form of rhymes and challenge them to guess the word that matches the clue. For example, "I have a long trunk, and I'm gray. I love to spray water and play. What am I?" (Answer: Elephant). Encourage them to come up with their own rhyming riddles to challenge family members or friends.

Remember, teaching phonics isn't just about decoding words - it's about creating a love for language, fostering imagination, and having a blast along the way!

As you can see from the activities listed, learning phonics skills can and should be fun for your child. There are also many other ways to encourage your child's letter/sound knowledge and phonics skills, such as alphabet songs, alphabet puzzles, ABC books and letter blocks. Providing a literacy-rich environment that allows your child to experience letters and sounds in many different ways is key in supporting your child's cognitive development.

*"Don't give up! I believe in you all.
A person's a person, no matter how small!*
-Dr. Seuss

5

Fun and Easy Fluency Activities

"Fluency is the bridge from decoding to comprehension."
-Informed Literacy

At the earliest stages of reading, children read slowly, focusing on decoding each word as they read. They are just trying to figure out the words, with little focus on the meaning of the words. A child at this stage of learning to read is not yet a fluent reader. However, when children are fluent readers, they are able to read the words automatically with speed and expression, which makes it easier for them to focus on the meaning of what they are reading. Most children become fluent readers by 7 or 8 years old. They know the words and are able to group them into meaningful phrases, which aids their understanding and comprehension. They are no longer focused on decoding words. They are now able to concentrate on what the words mean and use their prior knowledge to make connections to the text in a meaningful way.

In this book, I am focused on what parents can do to prepare their preschooler to be successful in school. So it might seem like reading fluency activities are for older children. That is true, but it is also true that there are many ways parents can help their child develop prereading skills that will greatly impact their later ability to read fluently. In this chapter, I will highlight several ways parents can support their child's reading readiness skills on their journey to becoming a fluent reader. These strategies include modeling fluent reading, supporting oral language development, and demonstrating print awareness activities.

In my opinion, the most effective way parents can help their child become a fluent reader is by modeling fluent reading. When you read aloud to your children, you help them to hear how fluent reading sounds. They are able to hear how you phrase words together and use intonation and expression as you read. Rereading favorite stories helps to make the words in the stories become familiar to your child and will help them build fluency in their ability to read those words.

Another important way to support the development of your child's reading fluency is to help them build strong oral language skills. Oral language encompasses both speaking and listening. Unlike reading, children learn to speak and communicate naturally and without formal instruction. Most kids enter school speaking and are able to communicate effectively. Research from the National Early Literacy Panel Report (2010) indicates "a strong correlation between oral language skills and reading success". Children who have strong oral language skills tend to learn to read easily. While children who have difficulties with speech tend to also have difficulties learning to read. Most preschool children have not learned to read yet, but they are building an oral language foundation that will support reading comprehension as they grow and learn. The article, "Oral Language Comprehension: Activities for Your Pre-K Child", suggests several fun and easy ways parents can help their child develop strong oral language skills.

*Walk and talk

When you take a walk through your neighborhood, encourage your child to point out things she sees and to talk about them. React to her observations, ask open-ended questions (who, what, why, where, when, how), and add your own observations to encourage a lively conversation. During the walk you might want to stop and say, "Listen, what can you hear?" Or if you hear a familiar sound, stop and say, "Do you hear that knocking sound? What do you think that could be? Maybe it's a woodpecker — let's look up and see if we can spot the bird."

*Act it Out

Read stories such as *The Three Bears* or *Three Billy Goats Gruff.* Act out the stories using different sized stuffed animals. This is a great opportunity to talk about the concept of "small, medium, and large". Go on a scavenger hunt in your home to find other objects of different sizes (shoes, socks, cups, etc.) and ask your child to classify the items by size. You might also ask your child if he knows another word for small and large.

*Sing it

Create or learn songs to expand your child's vocabulary. One idea: make up songs to describe your daily routines, periodically adding new verses that include new vocabulary words.

*Listening games

Play "I Spy" with your child using words that describe an object's position. ("I spy something on the carpet, in front of the couch, next to the dog.") Play games such as "Red-Light, Green-Light", "Mama, Puedo" and "Simon Says" that require talking, listening, following directions and giving directions.

*Kitchen conversations

Take advantage of daily activities. For example, while in the kitchen, encourage your child to name the utensils needed. Discuss the food you'll be eating, their color, texture, and taste. Where does the food come from? Which foods do you like? Which do you dislike? Who will clean up? Emphasize the use of prepositions by asking him or her to put the napkin on the table, in your lap, or under the spoon. Identify who the napkin belongs to: "It is my napkin." "It is Daddy's." "It is John's."

*We're going on an adventure
Ask your child to draw a map of an imaginary place he would like to explore. Have him tell you a little bit about the setting and who might live there. If you like, you can dress up (sometimes a hat or cardboard tube spyglass is all you need) and set out on your adventure. Encourage your child to tell you all about the journey and what he's experiencing. Your child will love it if you are "all in" for this imaginary journey!

*Tell me about it
After a read aloud, one of the best and easiest ways to check for understanding is to ask your child to summarize what the book was about in their own words. You can ask a question or two to help your child clarify her thinking or to add more detail.

*Family stories
This is a wonderful activity for a family picnic or for a rainy day when you're snuggled together on the couch. Share a favorite story about your childhood or a family story that's been passed down from generation to generation. Use vivid language and details about people, places, and things. Funny or scary will really get your child's attention! Your child will probably have lots of questions, which keeps the storytelling alive. You could also ask your child if she has a favorite family story of her own.

Building your child's print awareness skills is another way to promote reading fluency. Print awareness, which is also called "concepts of print", is a child's first introduction to literacy. This is when children begin to understand that print holds meaning and that the lines (letters) they see on the page represent speech sounds. Children are aware of print long before they go to school. They see it all around them; in books, on signs, on buildings and on television. Print awareness also helps them to understand how books work; how to hold the book, how to go from the top to bottom and left to right and how to turn the pages. Adults are fostering these skills when they point out letters and words to children. The article, "Print Awareness Activities for Your Pre-K Child" suggests several fun and easy ways to strengthen your child's print awareness skills.

*Introducing ...the book!

Very young children need to learn what a book is for, the different parts of a book, how to hold it, the purpose of the print and why we turn the pages.

Sit beside your child or hold him/her on your lap. Hold the book yourself or ask your child to hold the book, so she can learn how to properly handle a book. While holding it closed, point out the front cover, and then turn the book over and point out the back cover. Turn back to the front cover and read the title, moving your finger under each word as you read it. You can also ask your child to talk about the picture on the cover and tell you what they think the story might be about.

*Author, author

Point to the name of the author on the front of the book and tell your child that this is the person who thought of the story and wrote the words in the book. Then show your child the name of the illustrator and say that this is the person who created the drawings for the book. Sometimes the author is also the illustrator!

*Left to right, than turn the page

Tell your child, "I am going to read this page first and then this page over here next" Or "This is the top of the page. This is where I begin reading." Ask your child, "Do we begin reading from the front or the back of the book?" When you turn the page of a book, you can ask your child to show you where to begin reading on a page.

*The meaning of print

Point to words when reading with your child to show that print carries a message. For example, "Here are the penguin's words. He says,'thank you.'"

*What's a word?

Show your child that books are made up of letters that combine to form words. If your child is ready, point out some simple written words, say them aloud and talk about the match between spoken words and written words. For example, "Let's point to each word as I read it. Ready?"

*Follow my finger

When reading aloud, follow the words with your finger from left to right as you read them along with pointing to the pictures and any interesting details. As your emergent reader starts to read, they will learn to do the same thing.

*Introducing the alphabet

Point out individual letters in print and show how each letter has an uppercase and lowercase form. Help your child learn the names of each letter. For example, "This M on the red block is an uppercase letter. See how this uppercase letter is bigger than these lowercase letters?" There are lots of easy ways to help your child learn the letters of the alphabet, including the following:

- Read alphabet books to your child.
- Make alphabet cookies and say the individual letter names as you start to eat each one!
- If your child eats alphabet-shaped cereal or soup, point out the letters he eats, particularly the letters in the child's name.
- Make or buy alphabet letters and encourage your child to play with them.

*This book is full of letters!

This is a fun kind of alphabet search. Choose any picture book you might have in your home and have your child find each letter in the print. Your child may start by identifying letters randomly; later, your child can find the letters in alphabetical order. Look for lowercase and uppercase letters, too.

*License plate alphabet

As you take walks with your child, be on the lookout for letters of the alphabet on the cars in your neighborhood. You can start with trying to find the letters in your child's name. Make it even more challenging by trying to find all the letters from A to Z!

*Be a letter and word explorer!

Environmental print is the print of everyday life. This includes familiar symbols, words, and numbers found on signs, billboards, coupons, and stores. They are a natural way for children to learn that print carries meaning. Understanding that the big K means Kmart is a first step toward learning to read.

Cereal boxes are colorful and interesting to look at. Ask your child to find the first letter of his name somewhere on the box. See if he can find other letters from his name too. Cut out familiar words from cereal boxes, labels from soup cans and from yogurt containers. Use these individual words (Cheerios, tomato, Dannon) to talk about capital and lowercase letters. Talk about the sounds of letters ("The letter T says 'tuh' ").

This chapter highlighted many ways that parents can engage their preschool child in learning opportunities that will build reading readiness skills and set the stage for their ability to read fluently in later years. These activities should be fun and enjoyable for you and your child. The key is to simply embed them into your child's everyday life and help your child see that there are learning opportunities all around them. Children are naturally curious. Nurturing their curiosity is one of the most important ways to help your child become a lifelong learner.

Think left and think right and think low and think high.
Oh, the thinks you can think up if only you try!
-Dr Seuss

6

Fun and Easy Vocabulary Activities

Parents are the ultimate role models for children. Every word, movement and action has an effect. No other person or outside force has a greater influence on a child than the parent.
-*Bob Keeshan (Captain Kangaroo)*

A child's vocabulary impacts all areas of communication: speaking, listening, reading and writing. Did you know that the size of a child's vocabulary in kindergarten is a strong predictor of their ability to learn to read? It only makes sense that the more words they know and understand, the easier it is for them to comprehend what they are reading. The quote above illustrates the immense influence parents have on their children. You can have a great impact on your child's reading readiness just by having conversations with them. Talking to your child is a great way to increase your child's vocabulary.

According to Tracy Cutchlow, co-author, with John Medina, of Brain Rules for Baby: How to Raise a Smart and Happy Child from Zero to Five, "children who are spoken to more frequently in their first few years have IQs that are one-and-a-half times higher than those who aren't."

So as you can see, starting school with a strong vocabulary will have a great impact on your child's school success. The article, "Vocabulary: Activities for Your Pre-K Child" (https://www.readingrockets.org) suggests these fun and easy ways to increase your child's vocabulary.

- **Read aloud every day**

Reading aloud to your child and having your child read books on their own is the best way to increase their vocabulary. Books provide words they won't encounter in everyday conversations as the language of books is more complete and formal than talking. A great story also provides context and illustrations for learning a new word.

- **Bring in the nonfiction**

Nonfiction and informational books (such as the picture books by Gail Gibbons and Sneed Collard) offer young children a treasure chest of new and interesting words about our world. If the book has a glossary, spend some time discussing the words with your child, and as you read aloud, stop as often as needed to think about new words and how they connect to what your child already knows about.

- **Grocery store vocabulary**

Use the items on the grocery shelf to give your child practice finding something **above** their belly button, **below** their nose, on the **bottom** shelf, and **between** other items on a shelf. Opportunities to use superlatives, those little endings that help describe size, are all around the grocery store. Have your child find a big fruit, a bigger fruit and the biggest fruit in the produce section. What's the smallest item in the cart? The largest item?

- **Explore your world**

Visits to a museum, the zoo, the botanical garden, historical sites, and even your neighborhood park are terrific opportunities to introduce your child to new words. Spend some time looking at the signage and identifying new words, then connecting them to what you see right there.

In this chapter, I highlighted the crucial role that vocabulary plays in your child's success in learning to read and reading comprehension. Just by incorporating these simple conversation activities, you can greatly increase the size of your child's oral vocabulary which will have a huge impact on their reading comprehension and overall school success.

"Reading can take you places you have never been before."
— Dr. Seuss

7

Fun and Easy Comprehension Activities

*Don't just teach your children to read. Teach them to question what they read.
Teach them to question everything.* — George Carlin

Comprehension is the ultimate goal of reading. When a reader understands what they are reading, they are able to find joy and purpose in reading. However, reading is much more than just reading the words on the page. In order to comprehend what is being read, a child has to be an active reader. They need to focus on the text, make connections, ask questions and build a mental picture in their head of what they are reading. They need to build a sense of the story, or visualize, what is happening in their head as they read. There are many ways parents of preschoolers can set a foundation for reading comprehension for their future reader. In the article, "Comprehension: Activities for your Kindergartner" there are several fun and easy activities that are appropriate for preschool children, as well as, kindergartners.

- "I predict..."

FUN AND EASY COMPREHENSION ACTIVITIES

When you sit down for a read aloud, look at the book's cover together. Ask, "What do you think this book might be about? Why? Can you make some predictions?" Guide your child through the pages, discuss the pictures, and brainstorm what might happen in the story. Talk about any personal experiences your child may have that relate to the story.

- **Five-finger retell**

After reading a story together, have your child tell you five things about the story, using her fingers to talk about each one:

1. Characters: who was in the story?
2. Setting: where did the story take place?
3. Events: what happened in the story?
4. End: how did the story end?
5. Favorite character or part of the story.

- **Active reading**

Model active reading when you read with your child. Talk about what's happening as you're reading. Stop and discuss any interesting or tricky vocabulary words. Help your child make pictures of the story in his mind. Ask you child, "What just happened here? How do you think that character feels? Have you ever felt like that? What do you think will happen next?" Not only will this develop your child's comprehension, but critical thinking skills as well.

- **Mind movies**

When you come to a descriptive passage in a book, have your child close her eyes and create a mental movie of the scene. Encourage her to use all five senses. Read the passage over together, looking for details that bring the scene to life. Ask questions like, "How do you know it was a hot day? Which words help you understand that the child was lonely?"

- **Tell me about it**

After a read aloud, one of the best and easiest ways to check for understanding is to ask your child to summarize what the book was about in their own words. You can ask a question or two to help your child clarify her thinking or to add more detail.

This chapter highlighted ways you can help your child learn to think about reading and ask questions about what is being read. These simple activities are easy to incorporate into storytime with your child and will help your child develop strong reading comprehension skills. Comprehension is the final essential component in learning to read. It is an accumulation of all the first four components; phonological/phonemic awareness, phonics, fluency, and vocabulary. Each essential builds on each other in order to get to comprehension. If your child builds strong skills in each area, they will become a strong reader.

"The more that you read, the more things you will know. The more that you learn, the more places you'll go."
—Dr. Seuss

8

Building a Love of Reading and Learning

"There are many little ways to enlarge your child's world. Love of books is the best of all."
—*Jacqueline Kennedy*

In this final chapter, I would like to explore a few more important opportunities that will help to lay the groundwork for your child's school success and foster their love of books and learning. These activities will plant the seeds that will help your child grow into a lifelong learner.

Visiting the Library

Every year, I would take my first grade class on a field trip to the city library. They were so excited to see the children's library section. It was a magical place full of amazing things that children love, including puppet shows, learning toys, audiobooks, dress-up clothes for acting out stories, and so many books!

Taking your child to the library is a great way to encourage a love of reading. It is a place that can open the doors to so many new adventures and new learning. With shelves and shelves of books that span all subjects, your child is sure to find something they love. Best of all, everything is free to use at the library!

Most libraries have special programs and classes that your child can enjoy. Even toddlers and preschoolers can take part in storytime, as librarians dress up and act out the stories in a way that will thrill your child and bring the stories to life. Many libraries also have classes, such as arts and crafts, hands-on science exploration and cooking classes. Don't forget to sign your child up for the summer reading programs! In the article, "8 Tips for Visiting Your Local Library", Ellen Booth Church suggests these tips for unlocking the magic of the library that will nurture a lifelong love of learning:

1. **Set aside a special library time.** A regularly scheduled "date" gives children something to look forward to and helps you remember to keep it in your busy schedule. Mark these days on the calendar with a favorite color or sticker. When your child plots how many days she has to wait for the trip, she uses important sequencing and early reading skills.
2. **Arrange your visits around story time**, when a librarian (or visiting author) reads favorite children's books aloud. If you do this, select your books before the reading. The library is likely to be less crowded then, and the librarian will have more time to help if you need her.
3. **Meet the librarians.** Even if your child loves the library, she may initially be a little afraid of the people "in charge" of all those books. That's why it's important to introduce your child to the librarians. If they have time, librarians often like to give children a tour and help them get their first library card. This will allow your child to

foster a personal relationship, and the next time she arrives, she will see a familiar face.

4. **Teach your child how to care for books.** Children should learn at an early age not to harm or disrespect books. Teach the proper way to handle library property — no holding books with dirty hands, bending the cover or pages, scribbling, or tearing. Young readers need to understand the importance of protecting books so that everyone who uses the public library can enjoy them, again and again.

5. **Set limits and expectations.** Be clear about your guidelines for library time. Allow a specific amount of time for your child to explore, and set a limit on the number of books she can check out. Knowing your expectations ahead of time along with gentle reminders ("five minutes until we check out books") gives a budding book lover a comfortable structure to work within. You can point to the clock and draw on a piece of paper what the clock will look like when time is up. Or, set the alarm on your watch so that it goes off a few minutes beforehand. Don't worry too much about explaining rules, such as speaking quietly, at this point. Young children pick up the appropriate behavior very quickly, just by observing you.

6. **Share your child's passions.** Join in her excitement at discovering a book she likes, even if you don't think it's a great "take-home" book. Ask her what she finds interesting about it. Notice something about it to celebrate, whether it's the colors on the cover or the size of the book. Put the book in your pile, and then point out other books. When you get to the weeding-out process of choosing the three to take home, your child can finalize her choices.

7. **Snuggle up and read at the library.** Sharing a book in the library is a special occasion for children because they get to read in a novel

place surrounded by books! Find a cozy corner, or plop on the floor. This "pre-take-home" time also helps you and your child decide if a story is something she'll want to read again and again.
8. **Don't forget a book for you.** Borrow a book you're eager to read. This models a love of reading that will stay with your child her whole life. Since it's sometimes difficult to hunt down books, call ahead and see if the librarian can set aside a special book for you. That way, you can focus on your child while you're there, and she can really breathe in the beauty and peace and endless possibilities of library time.

Encouraging Imaginative Play

Children's imaginations grow very quickly during their first years of life. Imaginative play helps to strengthen their creative thinking skills and allows your child to connect to the world around them. Children love to play pretend games. Pretending to be a fireman or playing house or school helps children build social, emotional, physical and artistic skills. They learn to take turns, cooperate with others and expand their imaginations. They begin to see how they fit into the world around them.

Here are some ways to encourage pretend play:

- Stuffed animals
- Costumes
- Cardboard boxes
- Laundry baskets
- Kitchen sets and play foods
- Art supplies
- Exploring nature

- Music, songs and movement
- Musical instruments
- Blanket tents
- Making play dates with other children

Let your child take the lead and join in on the fun of pretending. It will help you understand your child's perspective of the world around them a little better and give you another great bonding experience.

"You're never too old, too wacky, too wild,
to pick up a book and read to a child."
-Dr. Seuss

9

Conclusion

My inspiration in writing this book came from my thirty years in an elementary classroom watching kids learn. I always questioned why learning seemed to come so easy to some students, while others struggled to learn. I have come to believe that the prior learning experiences that my students brought to school with them is what made all the difference. Some students were lucky enough to come from homes with literacy-rich environments where they were exposed to conversations and were read to from the time they were born. While other students' literacy exposure prior to school was very limited. As a result, they were lacking many of the reading readiness skills mentioned in this book. The difference in their readiness to learn truly made a difference in their ability to learn.

It is my goal that this book will give parents quality information and a variety of fun and easy activities, so that every parent can provide a literacy-rich environment for their child. I hope that every parent sees that by simply interacting with their child through books, conversations and play, it is possible for every child to come to school prepared to learn. That really is the magic that ignites the love of learning in your

CONCLUSION

child and empowers them to succeed in school and in life.

Thank you for reading my book, and I hope it empowers you with ideas and strategies that will help you nurture your child's mind, enhance their cognitive development and build a love of learning that will last their lifetime.

If you found this book helpful, I would be very appreciative if you left a favorable review on Amazon so that my book will be more visible to other parents like you.

10

References

8 Tips for Choosing Books for Kids. (n.d.). readingeggs.com. https://readingeggs.com/articles/2014-10-15-how-to-choose-books-for-kids/

Anderson, M. (2023, January 13). *Creative Ways to Incorporate Reading into Your Child's Daily Routine.* readsmartlearning.com. https://readsmartlearning.com/creative-ways-to-incorporate-reading-into-your-childs-daily-routine/

Phonological and Phonemic Awareness: Activities for Your Pre-K Child. (n.d.). readingrockets.org. https://www.readingrockets.org/literacy-home/reading-101-guide-parents/your-pre-kindergarten-child/phonological-and-phonemic

8 Fun Phonics Activities to do at Home. (n.d.). appbooka.com. https://appbooka.com/blog/teaching-phonics-at-home

Oral Language Comprehension: Activities for Your Pre-K Child. (n.d.). readingrockets.org. https://www.readingrockets.org/literacy-home/

REFERENCES

reading-101-guide-parents/your-pre-kindergarten-child/oral-language-comprehension

Print Awareness Activities for Your Pre-K Child. (n.d.). readingrockets.org. https://www.readingrockets.org/literacy-home/reading-101-guide-parents/your-pre-kindergarten-child/print-awareness-activities

Vocabulary: Activities for Your Pre-K Child. (n.d.). readingrockets.org. https://www.readingrockets.org/literacy-home/reading-101-guide-parents/your-pre-kindergarten-child/vocabulary-activities

Comprehension: Activities for Your Kindergartener. (n.d.). readingrockets.org. https://www.readingrockets.org/literacy-home/reading-101-guide-parents/your-kindergartener/comprehension-activities

Booth Church, E. (n.d.). *8 Tips for Visiting Your Local Library.* Scholastic.com. https://www.scholastic.com/parents/books-and-reading/reading-resources/developing-reading-skills/8-tips-visiting-your-local-library.html

About the Author

Debbie Forward, a retired educator with a deep passion for nurturing young minds, is also a dedicated mother who understands the joys and challenges of raising children. With a background in teaching and a heart full of parental wisdom, she has embarked on a mission to empower parents in their journey to help their children learn to read. Her experiences in the classroom and at home uniquely qualify her to guide parents through this crucial aspect of a child's development.

Made in the USA
Middletown, DE
19 March 2024